MY FIRST BOOK
NORTH KOREA

ALL ABOUT NORTH KOREA FOR KIDS

GLOBED
CHILDREN BOOKS

Interior and cover Design: Daniel Day
Editor: Margaret Bam

For My Sons, Daniel, David and Jude

Grand Monument, Mansu Hill, North Korea

North Korea

North Korea is a **country**.

A country is land that is controlled by a **single government**. Countries are also called **nations, states, or nation-states**.

Countries can be **different sizes**. Some countries are big and others are small.

Arch of Reunification, North Korea

Where Is North Korea?

North Korea is located in the continent of Asia.

A continent is a massive area of land that is separated from others by water or other natural features.

North Korea is situated in Eastern Asia.

Pyongyang, North Korea

Capital

The capital of North Korea is Pyongyang.

Pyongyang is located in the **western part** of the country.

Pyongyang is the largest city in North Korea.

Pyongyang, North Korea

Provinces

North Korea is a divided into 9 provinces

The provinces of North Korea are as follows:

Chagang, North Hamgyong, South Hamgyong, North Hwanghae, South Hwanghae, Kangwon, North Pyongan, South Pyongan, and Ryanggang

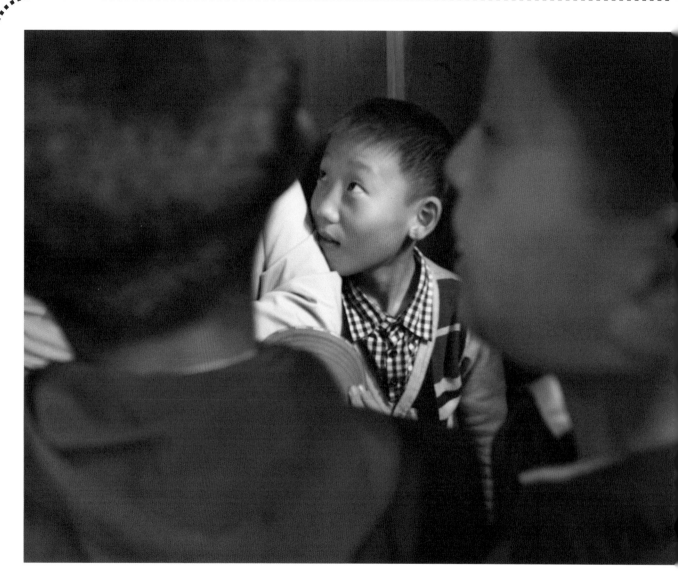

Metro, Subway, Pyongyang, North Korea

Population

North Korea has population of around **26 million people** making it the 55th most populated country in the world.

North Korea is known for its homogenous population, with over 98% of the population being ethnically Korean. The dominant ethnic group is the Korean people, who share a common language and cultural heritage.

Monument to Party Founding, Pyongyang, North Korea

Size

North Korea is **100210 square kilometres** making it the 98th largest country in the world by area.

North Korea has diverse landscapes, ranging from mountains and forests to plains and coastlines. North Korea borders China, Russia and South Korea.

Languages

The official language of North Korea is Korean. Munhwaŏ is the North Korean standard version of the Korean language.

Korean has around 80 million speakers.

Here are a few Korean phrases
- 안녕하세요 (ahn-nyung-ha-se-yo) — Hello
- 반갑습니다 (bahn-gap-seup-ni-da) — Nice to meet you
- 어떻게 지내세요? (uh-dduh-keh ji-neh-seh-yo?) — How are you?

Kim Il Sung Square

Attractions

There are lots of interesting places to see in North Korea.

Some beautiful places to visit in North Korea are

- Kim Il Sung Square
- Mansudae Hill Grand Monument
- Kumsusan Palace of the Sun
- Workers' Party Foundation Monument
- Grand People's Study House

Metro, Subway, Pyongyang, North Korea

History of North Korea

People have lived in North Korea for a very long time. In fact, it is believed that The Korean Peninsula was inhabited as far back as the Lower Paleolithic period. Its first kingdom was noted in Chinese records in the early 7th century BCE.

In 1948, Kim Il-sung, a prominent Korean leader, established the Democratic People's Republic of Korea (DPRK) and became its first leader. On 25 June 1950, North Korea invaded South Korea, and the Korean War began.

Kaesong, North Korea

Customs in North Korea

North Korea has many fascinating customs and traditions.

- Traditional Korean clothing, known as Hanbok, is still worn on special occasions in North Korea. The attire consists of a long, flowing robe called a chima for women, and a loose-fitting tunic called a jeogori for men. In everyday life, North Koreans typically wear Western-style clothing.
- Weddings in North Korea are typically held in a simple ceremony at a local government office, followed by a banquet with friends and family.

Music of North Korea

There are many different music genres in North Korea such as **Traditional Korean music, Pansori and Arirang.**

Some notable North Korean musicians include
- **Moranbong Band - North Korea's first girl band**
- **Hyon Song-wol - Leader of the Moranbong Band is often regarded as North Korea's biggest pop star.**

Kimchi

Food of North Korea

North Korea is known for having delicious, flavoursome and rich dishes.

The national dish of North Korea is **Kimchi** which is fermented cabbage and carrots in a delicious, tangy and spicy sauce.

Naengmyeon

Food of North Korea

North Korean cuisine is known for its unique flavours and influences from Korean and Chinese cooking.

Some popular dishes in North Korea include

- **Bulgogi: Thinly sliced marinated beef grilled to perfection, sweet and savoury.**
- **Pyongyang naengmyeon: Cold buckwheat noodles**
- **Naengmyeon: A cold noodle dish**
- **Jjigae: A stew made with various ingredients, such as tofu, seafood, meat, and vegetables.**

Pyongyang, North Korea

Weather in North Korea

North Korea has a **continental climate** with distinct four seasons. Winters can be harsh with cold temperatures and heavy snowfall, while summers are generally hot and humid.

The hottest month of the year in Pyongyang is August.

White-naped Crane

Animals of North Korea

There are many wonderful animals in North Korea.

Here are some animals that live in North Korea

- White-naped Crane
- Lynx
- Siberian Musk Deer
- Amur Leopard
- Korean Goral

The Juche Tower statue

Statues

There are many beautiful statues in North Korea which is one of the reasons why so many people visit this beautiful country every year.

Here are some of North Korea's statues

- The Chollima Statue
- The Victorious Fatherland Liberation War Museum Statue
- The Juche Tower statue
- Mansu Hill Grand monument

North Korean football

Sports of North Korea

Sports play an integral part in North Korea culture. The most popular sport is **Football.**

Here are some of famous sportspeople from North Korea

- **Sohn Kee-chung - Athletics**
- **Choe Chol-su - Boxing**
- **Om Yun-chol - Weightlifting**
- **Kim Un-guk - Weightlifting**

Kim Il-sung

Famous

Many successful people hail from North Korea.

Here are some notable North Korean figures

- **Kim Il-sung - The founder and first leader of North Korea**
- **Kim Jong-il - Former leader**
- **Kim Jong-un - Leader**
- **Yeonmi Park - Activist**
- **F.noah - TikTok Star**

Something Extra...

As a little something extra, we are going to share some lesser known facts about North Korea.

- Kim Il-sung, the country's founding leader, is highly revered in North Korea, and his birthday on April 15th is a national holiday.
- Traditional Korean martial arts, such as Taekwondo and Judo, are popular in the country.
- The Arirang Mass Games is a large-scale performance event held in North Korea, featuring synchronized gymnastics and dance.

Words From the Author

We hope that you enjoyed learning about the wonderful country of North Korea.

North Korea is a country rich in culture and beauty, with lots of wonderful places to visit and people to meet.

We hope you continue to learn more about this wonderful nation. If you enjoyed this book, consider leaving a review!

With Love

Printed in Great Britain
by Amazon

29462802R00027